# HELP ME, JESUS!

## PRAY STRONG THROUGH TOUGH TIMES

*Jason Nelson*

Published by Straight Talk Books
P.O. Box 301, Milwaukee, WI 53201
800.661.3311 · timeofgrace.org

Copyright © 2015 Time of Grace Ministry

All rights reserved. This publication may not be copied, photocopied, reproduced, translated, or converted to any electronic or machine-readable form in whole or in part, except for brief quotations, without prior written approval from Time of Grace Ministry.

Scripture is taken from THE HOLY BIBLE, NEW INTERNATIONAL VERSION®. NIV®. Copyright © 1973, 1978, 1984, 2011 by Biblica, Inc.® Used by permission. All rights reserved worldwide.

Printed in the United States of America
ISBN: 978-1-942107-86-6

TIME OF GRACE *and* IT ALL STARTS NOW *are registered marks of Time of Grace Ministry.*

*I was pouring out my soul to the LORD.... I have been praying here out of my great anguish and grief.*

1 SAMUEL 1:15,16

# Introduction

Prayer changes things. It does. It changes the mind of God. There is plenty of biblical evidence for that. Our prayers engage God's intentions. He is responsive to our requests while still being God. He listens attentively to each of us and considers in an almighty way what he will do to alter difficult circumstances or bolster us so that we can get through them.

Prayer also changes our mind-set. We think about God when we pray to him. We think better about others when we are praying for them. We shrink overwhelming circumstances when we get our minds around them so we can express ourselves to God.

We don't have to mince words with God or wait until we figure out how to put it to him. Just put it to him spirit to spirit with groans, sighs, tears, fears, and expectations. Prayer is dialogue with God when we remind him of his promises that circle back to strengthen our faith and give us hope.

You can find your own way to pray, but pray strong through tough times. Pray loud when you need to. Pray soft when you want to. Pray often like it's breathing. Pray in Jesus' name. He prayed too, and he loves you.

# Help me, Jesus, never give up

*Those who hope in the L*ORD *will renew their strength.*
Isaiah 40:31

Lord, I want to crawl back into bed, pull the covers over my head, and stay there. I don't think I can take it anymore. I just want to quit everything. The sad reality is I'm not sure anyone would notice. Everyone else would go on their merry way. You said you wouldn't give me more than I can handle. Maybe.

I could handle life better if the problems didn't come all at once. It's one set back after another. Just when I think I have it under control, here's one more thing I didn't see coming. But you did. And you let it through. What are you thinking? I don't have anything left. You should know that. You're in the loop here because you're God. You must see something in me that I don't. You must see a way to cope that I'm missing. Help me discover that. Help me figure out how to keep going.

I'll try one more day, sweet Jesus. Maybe that's the key. One more day. If I can get one problem solved today it will get easier, especially if it's the critical one. If I can just get through today. . . . But I can only do it with you at my side. I don't want to give up.

I thought about poor Job today. It was one thing after another for him too. But he didn't blame you. He took it for granted that our days could be full of trouble. When he hated his life, he loved you more. When he just wanted to die, he looked toward heaven. He didn't give up, and you didn't give up on him. So I asked myself, "Has God ever let me down?" The answer is, never. I have had major problems in the past, but I'm still here and they are distant memories.

My present troubles will also fade into the background. I know that my Redeemer is alive and well, and I will be too. Amen.

**Reflections:**

_____
_____
_____
_____
_____

**Personal prayers:**

_____
_____
_____
_____
_____

# Help me, Jesus, bring up my children

*Start children off on the way they should go,*
*and even when they are old they will not turn from it.*
Proverbs 22:6

God Almighty, what is wrong with my kids? They just won't listen. You say they're a blessing. Well, today I'm sorry I had any of them. I don't know if they're full of sugar or possessed by demons.

Where is a pirate ship when I need one? I would sell every one of them. Well, maybe not the baby, but the rest for sure. I know that's crazy talk, but they are making me that way. I'm tempted to toss them an iPad and tell them to leave me alone. As long as I can keep the lid on, what difference does it make?

But they need discipline. They need to learn to control themselves. I need to learn to control myself. The last thing hyper children need is an agitated parent.

Lord, help me be calm and get my children's attention so that I can raise them right. They need to do what I say, and yelling just isn't working. I'm afraid it's making them worse.

Shhh, Lord. They are finally asleep. If some loud noise wakes them up, that's on you. I can't deal with it. They need some rest. I need some rest. Please give us some rest.

I've seen pictures of you with children, Lord. They're crawling in your lap. You don't seem bothered that they're hanging on you. They look well behaved and happy. Mine look like angels when they're sleeping. That's when I think I see what you see in them. I know how much you love them. You know how much I love them.

Please give me your strength, your patience, your endurance, and more than anything, your love so I can show it to them. I want to do the right things and say the right things. I want to be a good parent. Forgive my frustration. Help me be the adult around here. Give all of us a good night's rest. I want to do better tomorrow. I want to repair any damage I've caused and build them up. Amen.

**Reflections:**

_____

_____

_____

_____

**Personal prayers:**

_____

_____

_____

_____

# Help me, Jesus, live with pain

*But as for me, afflicted and in pain—*
*may your salvation, God, protect me.*
Psalm 69:29

Lamb of God, you take away the sin of the world. Please do something about my pain. I don't remember the last time I felt good. Oh, I wear a smile and try to act normal. Sometimes I disguise a limp. I've learned to push through pain to get things done and be part of activities.

I'm no hero, Lord. I just have no choice, and I'm weary of it. I've been around those who preach the benefits of suffering; how it produces character and all that. But I suspect they haven't suffered much or they wouldn't be so glib. It's like poverty. It seems quaint until you become poor.

You've noticed I don't pray much about it anymore because nothing seems to change. It's there day after day. I'm sorry for talking to you like this. I know you are still at work in my life. But I'm very tired of pain.

Jesus, you and I have something in common. It's a cross. It's a very rugged cross. You didn't want yours, and I don't like mine.

But because you carried yours, I can live with mine. You went to your cross and turned suffering on its head. Grace was in your pain. Eternal life came out of your death. You made your cross my way of salvation. Now I ask you to make my cross a way for me to serve others. Use my pain to make me more compassionate. Use my pain to make me more sensitive to what others are going through. Use my pain to crucify any self-righteousness in me so that I can be accessible and trustworthy when someone needs my help.

I guess I don't need to be pain free, but I need to be able to endure it. Lord, if you're not going to take my pain away, then please make good use of it. Amen.

**Reflections:**

_____

_____

_____

_____

_____

**Personal prayers:**

_____

_____

_____

_____

_____

# Help me, Jesus, give it time

*Be still before the Lord and wait patiently for him.*
Psalm 37:7

God, I don't know what's wrong with me. I have no patience anymore. There is lava boiling inside me, and it's always ready to erupt.

Little things set me off. See that lady with the cart ahead of me. She has no clue I'm trying to get past her to get some creamed corn. She's digging around in her purse looking for something she can't seem to find and is oblivious to the traffic jam she has caused in this aisle. Today I'm so irritable that I would pay someone to take her out. That's a terrible thought. She's probably a very nice person.

But I'm always ready to explode. I'm always wound too tight. I'm always impatient and cranky with people around me just because they are there. That's no way to be, Lord. I'm going to say something to someone that I'll regret.

I need to go somewhere and decompress. I need to get away. Will you come with me, Jesus? Better yet, will you lead me somewhere peaceful? Please be a gentle shepherd and make me a gentler person. Take me to still waters, to green pastures, and to serenity. Put me in a vespers state of mind and calm my soul. Let me meditate on your Word like I do when evening falls and light grows dim. Let me kneel and offer a long thoughtful prayer without any distractions.

Lord, I need to be in a quiet church or on a hillside to watch the sun go all the way down. I need to be anywhere I can't hurry and where there aren't any annoying people. I need to stay there for as long as it takes. Everything else can wait. Teach me how to wait and be calm about it. Please wait with me. Amen.

**Reflections:**

_____
_____
_____
_____
_____
_____

**Personal prayers:**

_____
_____
_____
_____
_____
_____

# Help me, Jesus, reclaim our love

*I will give you a new heart and put a new spirit in you; I will remove from you your heart of stone and give you a heart of flesh.*
Ezekiel 36:26

What happened to us, Lord? We live under the same roof but that's about it. We don't sleep in the same bed anymore and rarely make love. Our lives together started out great. We spent time doing things we both enjoyed. We made each other happy. We raised our children together. We talked.

Now we hardly look at each other. We do our own thing and go our separate ways. I guess the arguments took their toll. The name-calling hurt both of us. Leaving things unresolved made us indifferent to each other. I hate this, but somehow we got used to it being this way. Now the distance between us is normal. It would feel awkward to bring up our relationship. But even an argument would show we still matter to each other.

What can we do to close the gap, Lord? Do we even want to close the gap? Maybe we should face the facts and get divorced.

Jesus, please help us fall in love again. I don't want to give up on our marriage. Give us the courage to break the silence and actually communicate. Help us get to know each other all over again and look at each other affectionately. We made a commitment in front of you that this marriage would last as long as we do. We need to start talking about it calmly and not blame each other for drifting apart. We need to ask each other for forgiveness. We need to forgive each other as you have forgiven us. We need to create a better story of *us*.

Could you help us say those words to each other that were easy to say years ago? I think we still love each other, and we need to say it. And we both love you, Jesus. Please help us reclaim our love for each other. Amen.

**Reflections:**

_____

_____

_____

_____

_____

**Personal prayers:**

_____

_____

_____

_____

# Help me, Jesus, be positive

*Let your gentleness be evident to all. The Lord is near.*
Philippians 4:5

Lord of heaven and earth, this world is choking on negativity. I'm ready to cancel cable TV because I'm tired of being inundated with commentary by pessimistic people. It's the nagging tone of our politics, and it casts a dark shadow over too much programming. I guess it's only newsworthy today if it can be covered by a naysayer. Whatever happened to objectivity and wishing people better tomorrows?

It's amazing how many "experts" agree that we are headed for the unraveling of a nice life as we know it. I want to gag every time someone predicts another Armageddon. Then it carries over at work. People don't keep their philosophies to themselves. They gripe about everything that's going on, using the same rants as the knuckleheads on talk radio. Negativity has a very large audience. It's a trap that I don't want to fall into, but I think I just did.

Let me push back in a positive way, but I can't react to everything. Lord, don't you think it's best if I don't say too much? Maybe that will get noticed. And when I do chime in, help me be constructive.

Let me offer folks a better way of looking at things without being antagonistic or sounding naive.

For me to stay positive, dear Jesus, I need to be exposed to positive things. You are light. Nothing is more positive than your gospel. Nothing is more uplifting than your love and the promises in your Word. This world needs that light, and I want to be a big candle.

Help me keep my resolve, Lord. Give me your Holy Spirit so that I can have a good attitude most of the time. I want my faith and my optimism to be taken seriously by others. I want to be a positive influence on them and change the world. Amen.

**Reflections:**

_____
_____
_____
_____
_____

**Personal prayers:**

_____
_____
_____
_____

# Help me, Jesus, face death

*Blessed are the dead who die in the Lord.*
Revelation 14:13

I need a miracle, Lord. I'm devastated knowing that's what it would take to keep me alive. I've asked for miraculous healing for others. But I never thought it would be necessary for me.

At first I thought my doctor was being overly conscientious. I didn't feel that sick. I thought she was ordering all those tests to be on the safe side. I wondered if she was overdoing it. But the results confirmed her suspicions. I'm very ill and will die soon. It hurt her to tell me. And I'm starting to feel it. It's progressing. There is no treatment that will make a difference, so I'm not going to bother with any.

But I will accept a miracle if you have one for me, because I'm not ready for this. I don't want to die. I like my life, and I love the people in it. I don't know how to accept the end.

Now I know what it feels like when life slips away. I've watched others die, and now I know for myself. I'm frightened and I'm sad. There are heroes of faith who were able to console others from their deathbeds. I don't know if I can be one of them. My loved ones are crying, and I am too. But I do believe in you, Jesus. I believe with all my heart you died for me. And when my heart stops beating, I have no doubt I will be with you in heaven.

Please keep Satan away as the end draws nearer. I don't want to become confused during my own death. Be with those who are taking care of me as I pass. Comfort me and bless them.

When it finally goes dark and quiet and cold, let me quickly hear the rustling of angels, feel your warmth, and see the face of God. Amen.

**Reflections:**

_____
_____
_____
_____
_____
_____
_____

**Personal prayers:**

_____
_____
_____
_____
_____
_____

# Help me, Jesus, save my son

*How can a young person stay on the path of purity?*
*By living according to your word.*
Psalm 119:9

What is it about young men today? So many of them are anxious and angry. So many of them are reckless and in trouble. We are losing too many young men. I remember the day I held my son over the font and the pastor touched his head three times with wet fingers and put your name on him. There were promises made and expectations established. He got off to such a good start and was a very good boy. Everything we expected. There were promises with that water but no guarantees.

I hate the drugs! They wreck a young man's brain. And the drug dealers! They look for the weak and sell them poison. People say he needs tough love. Well, loving him is very tough. People say he needs to hit bottom. The bottom is death, and I don't want to lose my son.

I know you heard him barge out of here. There was screaming and profanity. I made him accountable and insisted he get help. He was furious with me.

The days have turned into weeks. I don't know where he spends the nights. I don't know if he has anything to eat. If I sleep at all, I wake with the same dread. My stomach is in a knot every time the phone rings. It could be him. It could be someone calling about him. This is a nightmare.

O Lord, send angels to protect him. Send your Holy Spirit to soften his resentment and restore memories of your love, how he was raised, and his family's love. Send people into his life to help him. Make him ready to change his ways. I know you can do it, Jesus. You can walk across the water and take hold of my son before he goes all the way under. Amen.

**Reflections:**

_____
_____
_____
_____
_____
_____

**Personal prayers:**

_____
_____
_____
_____
_____
_____

# Help me, Jesus, respect the power of money

*Whoever gathers money little by little makes it grow.*
Proverbs 13:11

You are a generous friend, Jesus. In one way or another, you have given us everything we have. Thank you for all of it.

But I wish someone would have taught me about money when I was young. I would have more today. No one told me that money always goes where it is treated the best. I learned the hard way that it evaporates without a trace whenever we waste it or use it foolishly. Who knows what I even spent it on? Poof. But it grows impressively when we manage it shrewdly, just like you said it would.

Sure, I grew up hearing that loving money too much could lead to all kinds of evil. I know that money can own us if our priorities are off. But no one ever mentioned that if I invested it wisely, I would have more of it and could do more good with it. And if they did, I didn't listen.

Jesus, would you agree that it's never too late to make better use of our money? I think you would. You expressed great appreciation for what the widow did with her last little shekels. You allowed a wealthy benefactor to pay for your grave. Your group kept a small treasury so you could get the things you needed, but it was in the hands of the wrong person.

Money makes a big difference in our lives. It's just a fact. You gave it power. If we don't have enough, we lose our independence and our dignity. When we have enough, we can take care of ourselves and hold our heads high. And when we have more than enough, we can help others and support your church.

Help me respect the power of money, Lord. Bless my investments like you did for Abraham. Let me do well so that I can do much more good. Amen.

**Reflections:**

_____
_____
_____
_____
_____
_____

**Personal prayers:**

_____
_____
_____
_____
_____
_____

# Help me, Jesus, banish my shame

*Instead of your shame you will receive a double portion, and instead of disgrace you will rejoice in your inheritance.*
Isaiah 61:7

Precious Savior, forgive my unbelief. That is exactly what it was. It was unbelief because I knew it was wrong and went with it anyway. I planned it out, acted with forethought, and told my conscience to keep quiet. My intentions were wrong from the beginning. I never expected I would get caught. I covered my tracks and deleted what I needed to delete. There were no records, no receipts, and no witnesses.

Somehow, I was careless because I got caught. Is this your love at work? Were you behind this? Did you call me out publicly so I would stop and repent of my sin? Now everyone knows, and I am so ashamed of myself. I ruined my own reputation. My family must be ashamed too because I degraded our good name. I feel totally exposed and have nowhere to hide. I hate myself for doing this. I can't imagine how disappointed you are, but I need to hide in you.

Precious Savior, I know you love me because I got caught. How do I start to put this behind me? There are consequences, and it's going to take time for me to pay my dues. I admit my sin and make no excuses. I am sorry. And if there's a stronger word for it, I'm that too.

Please forgive me and please move others to forgive me. I want to begin the long, slow process of rebuilding my reputation. I must be humble every day because this will always be a blemish on my record. I'm asking for a second chance because that's the kind of God you are.

Fill me with your Spirit and work in me so that it is clear to everyone that your forgiveness wasn't wasted on me. I want people to trust me again, but just saying so would be suspicious. Help me earn it with every fiber of my being. Amen.

**Reflections:**

_____
_____
_____
_____
_____

**Personal prayers:**

_____
_____
_____
_____

# Help me, Jesus, stay safe

*Don't be afraid.... Those who are with us
are more than those who are with them.*
2 Kings 6:16

Wow, this world is a dangerous place. There are crazy people with guns and crazy people with bombs. It doesn't seem like more guns and bombs is the answer. Violence breeds violence. Innocent people get hurt just because they were in the wrong place at the wrong time.

How do I protect myself? How do I keep my family safe? I don't want to turn home sweet home into some kind of fortress. I refuse to assemble a small arsenal so I can hold up my end of a shoot-out. I don't want to live in fear and be paranoid. Safety is a blessing of liberty. I want to be safe in my home. I want to be safe walking the streets. I want to be safe traveling this great land. I know we have to take precautions and keep our eyes open for danger. That is the beginning of self-defense. But, Jesus, where does it end?

I would feel safer, Jesus, if I could see the fighting angels who are guarding me. I would feel safer if I could see their blazing chariots and lightning swords defending me. I would feel better if I could see the steel in their eyes as they watch for danger. You say they surround us and protect us, and I believe you. They've done a good job so far. I ask you to also deploy their human allies to keep us safe.

Bless the police officers and firefighters who risk their lives for us. Bless our soldiers and intelligence agencies that are watching over us along with the angels. Bless those who investigate crimes and apprehend criminals before they can harm others. Make public safety a priority in our nation and give us the best public servants to provide it. Make us law-abiding people who look out for each other and keep one another safe. Amen.

**Reflections:**

_____

_____

_____

_____

**Personal prayers:**

_____

_____

_____

_____

# Help me, Jesus, have an encore

*See, I am doing a new thing! Now it springs up;
do you not perceive it? I am making a way in the
wilderness and streams in the wasteland.*
Isaiah 43:19

Unbelievable! After all these years, I got the dreaded pink slip. Well, it was on white paper, but the message was clear: "Due to necessary restructuring, we regret to inform you that we no longer need your services. This is effective immediately. Thank you for your time with our company." I just got shot out of the company cannon into the great unknown.

Now what will I do, Lord? I don't even want to tell my family. They'll be devastated. I feel very insecure. Is this how loyalty gets rewarded? I worked hard and long and didn't complain when I was asked to do more. And now this? I'm so mad. I have a feeling when I'm done being mad, I'm going to be scared. What will I do? This job is all I know. The economy isn't clamoring for people like me. I need income, and I need it fast.

Well, Lord, I've posted my résumé. I've searched for openings online and in the papers. I've made cold calls and filled out applications. I'm waiting for an interview, and the bills are piling up.

Lord, please help me find the job you have picked out for me. I'm having trouble pushing myself because I'm getting discouraged. I just can't be washed up. I need a job, and I'm willing to try something new. I'm willing to put my experience and skills to work in an unexpected way. It would be energizing and fun to be surprised with a novel career. I could get a second wind.

Give me some imagination, Jesus. Let me see where the opportunities really are and give me the resourcefulness to pursue them. I love you, Jesus. You promised that no matter what, you will work for my good. I'm looking forward to the day I can look back and see what it is because I am working too. Amen.

**Reflections:**

_____
_____
_____
_____

**Personal prayers:**

_____
_____
_____
_____

# Help me, Jesus, forgive all of them

*With you there is forgiveness,
so that we can, with reverence, serve you.*
Psalm 130:4

I don't mind forgiving people, Jesus. I'm just rather selective about it. If a careless person steps on my toe and says he's sorry, I forgive him right away. Not a problem. If someone unintentionally harms me and then tries to make it right, I am very gracious about it. I can deal with inconvenience due to circumstances beyond anyone's control.

But I struggle to forgive people who have unjustly hurt me. I struggle to forgive people who should know better. I struggle when there was no reason for their criticism or resentment. I admit I hold grudges. I sentence people to the ice-cold hell of the unforgiven in my very long memory. And the place is filling up. Thinking about them makes me so bitter I can taste it. They have a miserable hold on me because I can't forgive them. And the bigger problem is that I regularly ask you to forgive me as I forgive others.

Jesus, how could you hang there and ask God to forgive them? I get it with the criminal hanging next to you. He seemed sorry and asked you to remember him. I understand how you could overlook your disciples' shortcomings and forgive the mistakes they made along the way. I suppose you thought the soldiers were just doing their jobs and the mob got caught up in hysteria when they shouted, "Crucify him!"

But how could you ask God to forgive the Sanhedrin that was looking for false evidence against you? How could you ask God to forgive Pontius Pilate, who was playing politics with your life? They should have known better. But forgiveness was the reason you were hanging on that cross, and withholding it from anyone is not in your character. Forgiving all of them unburdened your human spirit and let your godliness shine through. Forgiveness was your great victory. Let me honor it by forgiving all of them. Amen.

**Reflections:**

_____
_____
_____
_____

**Personal prayers:**

_____
_____
_____

# Help me, Jesus, be glad for church

*I rejoiced with those who said to me,*
*"Let us go to the house of the Lord."*
Psalm 122:1

Some days, Lord, I feel like an imposter. I've been a churchgoer for a long time. I was raised in the church. I participated in all of the programs. I know most of the right answers and can dish them out.

Most Sundays I'm really not hearing anything new. Am I just keeping up appearances? I go more out of habit and less out of conviction. I know it's a good habit, and I don't think I want to break it. It makes my parents happy when I go. But sometimes my heart just isn't in it. And I want my heart to be in it. There have been stretches where I don't go, and the longer I'm away the easier it is to stay away. It's not because I want to sleep in or have other things to do. It's because I've lost interest. It's just not a priority for me. I'm missing the connection between going to church and being a Christian.

You know I've met someone, Lord. It's going well and we could get married. Now I think we should go to church together. Isn't that weird? When I was single, it wasn't always that important. But now that there's someone else in my life, I think we should go. I want to get married in the church. I want to raise my children in the church. I want it to be a big part of our lives together like it was when I was growing up.

Having someone to be in church with seems to make a difference. Maybe that's the whole point of church. It's a gathering of people who believe in you and support one another. When I went alone, I felt isolated and it didn't mean as much. But when I feel the connection to you and those around me, it means more. I guess I had the focus wrong. It was on me.

Let me refocus on you, Lord Jesus, and appreciate everyone around me. Amen.

**Reflections:**

_____

_____

_____

**Personal prayers:**

_____

_____

_____

# Help me, Jesus, find strength in you

*Be strong in the grace that is in Christ Jesus.*
2 Timothy 2:1

Don't let the swagger fool you, Lord. I'm not that sure about anything. I wish it was socially acceptable to admit weakness. I talk like I know what I'm talking about. I act like I know what I'm doing. I'd lose my job if I didn't and probably most of my friends. But the truth is, I feel a regular uneasiness about myself, and I'm afraid to admit it.

I'm not happy with me. And it's hard to put into words. I doubt my ability. I second-guess my decisions. When I'm with others, I feel inadequate because they seem so sure of themselves. I give myself pep talks and try to convince myself I bring something to the table that others don't. But it feels like I'm rationalizing being a failure. It's an odd thing, Lord, because I'm not even sure why I feel this way. I can't put my finger on it.

Jesus, I have concluded that creeping self-doubt is the silent killer of happiness. I'm not looking to be all that. I would just like to have a little more self-assurance.

It helps me to remember you accomplished a lot with weak people. Moses made excuses. Jonah headed the other way. And Paul was hostile at first.

The thing they had in common was you, Lord. They found their strength in you. I don't want to be something I'm not but would like to be happy about everything I am. I know you were very careful when you created me. You didn't throw me together with spare parts but knit me together to be unique in every way. You spared nothing in your sacrifice to make me your child and give me salvation.

You have given me every reason to be confident in this life. This is a spiritual struggle for me, Lord. Help me find my strength in you. Amen.

**Reflections:**

_____
_____
_____
_____
_____
_____

**Personal prayers:**

_____
_____
_____
_____
_____

# Afterward

An extraordinary thing happened because I was asked to write these prayers. I couldn't stop praying. I found myself doing it everywhere, all the time. I prayed better than I usually do because I had to. I had to confront some of the tough issues we all face and tune my thoughts toward God's ears so I could put words on paper. Don't hesitate to try it yourself. And when I had to step away, I couldn't wait to get back at it because I had one more thing to say. I learned a lot about praying by writing these prayers and was blessed because I got to say them first. May they be a blessing to you.

This is the confidence we have in approaching God: that if we ask anything according to his will, he hears us.

1 JOHN 5:14

# About the Writer

**Jason Nelson** had a career as a teacher, counselor, and leader. He has a bachelor's degree in education, did graduate work in theology, and has a master's degree in counseling psychology. After his career ended in disabling back pain, he wrote the book *Miserable Joy: Chronic Pain in the Christian Life* (2007, Northwestern Publishing House). He has written and spoken extensively on a variety of topics related to the Christian life. Jason lives with his wife, Nancy, in Wisconsin.

## About Time of Grace

Time of Grace is for people who want more growth and less struggle in their spiritual walk. Through the timeless truth of God's Word, we connect people to God's grace so they know they are loved and forgiven and so they can start living in the freedom they've always wanted.

To discover more, please visit timeofgrace.org or call 800.661.3311.

## Help share God's message of grace!

Every gift you give helps Time of Grace reach people around the world with the good news of Jesus. Your generosity and prayer support take the gospel of grace to others through our ministry outreach and help them find the restart with Jesus they need.

**Give today at timeofgrace.org/give or by calling 800.661.3311.**

Thank you!